METAL LEGENDS ALPHABET

Words by Robin Feiner

A is for **A**nthrax.
Out of Queens, New York, Anthrax was formed in 1981 by goateed guitarist Scott Ian. Nominated for six Grammys, they love fast, heavy riffs with a generous dose of fun. Alongside Metallica, Slayer, and Megadeth, they're one of the 'Big Four' of thrash metal.

B is for **B**lack Sabbath. Formed in England in '68, these legends are recognized as the first heavy metal band. After cutting the irrepressible Ozzy Osbourne, Tony Iommi was joined up front by the equally legendary Ronnie Dio. These Rock and Roll Hall of Famers are one of the most influential bands ever.

C is for Mötley Crüe.
With big riffs and bigger hair, Mötley Crüe has mixed glam and heavy metal to kickstart your heart since 1981. From Los Angeles' wild Sunset Strip, they're known as much for partying as for their epic live shows where legendary drummer Tommy Lee plays while riding a rollercoaster!

D is for **D**ream Theater.
In 1985, Dream Theater formed in Boston and quickly became one of the 'Big Three' of progressive metal alongside Queensrÿche and Fates Warning. These headbangers have sold over 12 million records and received three Grammy nominations, including a win for The Alien.

E is for Exodus.
These thrashers are known as 'kings of the Bay Area scene'—a title they share with Metallica. Exodus formed in 1979 and, thanks to unrelenting reinvention, is still going strong today. Their mix of metal and punk on Fabulous Disaster and Tempo of the Damned makes for a turbulent and toxic waltz.

F is for Mercyful **F**ate.
Out of the ashes of punk
band Brats, Mercyful Fate
formed in Denmark in 1981.
With enigmatic King Diamond
center stage and wearing
ghoulish 'corpse paint,' the
band created a black metal
sound that influenced many
giants of the genre.

G is for **G**irlschool. Forming during the New Wave of British Heavy Metal (NWOBHM), these chicks with a worldwide cult following have been headbanging since 1978. That earns them the legendary status of being the longest-running all-female rock band! An inspiration to female rock musicians, their 'punk-tinged metal' will live forever.

H is for **H**elloween.
The 'fathers of power metal'
exploded onto the German
scene in 1984 and never looked
back. Despite a revolving
door of members and shared
vocal duties, these legends
have been honored with 14
gold and six platinum records.

I is for **I**ron Maiden. Playing fast and furious, these English lads flew the flag for the NWOBHM era in the '80s. Live, their theatrics and visuals are infamous, thanks to their gruesome mascot Eddie. An icon in the genre, he appears on their albums, T-shirts, and even pinball machines!

J is for Judas Priest.
These bad boys from
Birmingham have been
breaking the law—breaking
the law for more than 50 years,
selling over 50 million albums,
and winning a Grammy.
Leading the charge is the
silver-studded Rob Halford,
whose legendary falsetto set
the standard for metal singers.

K is for **K**orn.
When it comes to Nu metal, we've all been following the leader Korn. Ever since forming in the early '90s, they've been playing slow, deep, and heavy with a hint of hip-hop, earning themselves a couple of well-deserved Grammys. These freaks on a leash are one of metal's most legendary bands.

L is for **L**amb of God.
Out of Richmond, Virginia, Lamb of God quickly laid to rest any doubt about their sheer power with their debut album, New American Gospel. Seven albums later, their jagged riffs, rapid-fire drums, and monstrous vocals carry the groove metal torch that Pantera left behind.

Mm

M is for Metallica.
1981 saw the birth of what would ultimately become the biggest metal band of all time! Like some kind of ravenous monster, these Hall of Fame inductees have won eight Grammys, sold over 125 million albums, and are widely considered one of the greatest bands of all time. True legends.

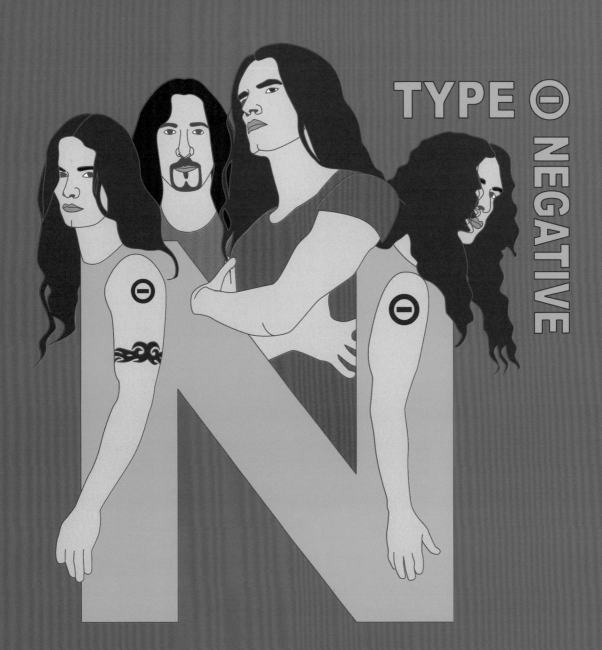

TYPE ⊖ NEGATIVE

N is for Type O **N**egative. With Black Sabbath and the Beatles as influences, these boys from Brooklyn certainly earned the nickname 'The Drab Four.' In 1991, they defined gothic metal with their debut album, Slow, Deep and Hard, and followed it up with the platinum Bloody Kisses. Sadly, these legends disbanded in 2010.

Oo

O is for **O**peth.
Mixing Nordic folk with death metal, this progressive outfit from Stockholm, Sweden, evokes the cold of Scandinavia. Formed in 1989, they've released 13 studio albums, including 2019's In Cauda Venenum—recorded and released in both Swedish and English to rave reviews.

P is for Pantera.
These cowboys from Texas went from '80s glam metal to a new level by enlisting the deep growl of Phil Anselmo. Brutal and raw, Pantera demonstrated a vulgar display of power that inspired a new generation of groove metal bands like Korn and Lamb of God before breaking up in 2003.

Q is for **Q**ueensrÿche.
One of the defining acts
of progressive metal,
Queensrÿche found huge
success with 1988's concept
album Operation Mindcrime.
Tours with Guns N' Roses and
Metallica followed. Dubbed
the 'thinking man's metal,'
their music is complex and
addresses important
social issues.

R is for **R**ammstein.
As if metal wasn't forceful enough, Germany's Rammstein, or 'Ramming Stone,' arrived in the mid-1990s. Despite singing mostly in German, their brand of industrial metal carved them a global niche. In 2019, their seventh album, Rammstein, reached No. 1 in 14 countries.

S is for Slayer.
Another of the genre-defining 'Big Four' thrash bands, Slayer formed in Los Angeles in 1981. Their gory, horror-filled lyrics were met not only with album bans and lawsuits but also four certified gold records and two Grammys! After nearly 40 legendary years, the band retired in 2019.

T is for Tool.
The more traditional heavy metal sounds on their demo, 72826, transitioned into a defining mix of progressive and alternative metal on the Grammy-winning Ænema. Since then, these legends from LA with a hatred for music streaming services have won another two Grammys.

U is for Underoath.
Plucking their name 'from somewhere in the Bible,' these Grammy-nominated screamers helped shape Metalcore, a mix of metal and hardcore punk. After disbanding in 2013, they reunited and have released two more cracking albums.

V is for **V**enom.
Formed in the '70s, this
British band is credited as
a major influence on thrash
and extreme metal. Referring
to their first album, Lars Ulrich
explained, 'Venom started
it all with one record.' Their
second album—Black Metal—
has since become the name
of the genre.

Ww

W is for **W.**A.S.P.
These classic West Coast metalheads formed in Los Angeles in 1982 and still rock 40 years on. Known for their wild antics and shocking lyrics, they infamously fought back against the Parents Music Resource Center, a group who targeted risqué music, with their single Harder Faster.

Xx

X is for Symphony X. Founded in 1994, New Jersey's Symphony X, as the name suggests, embraced neoclassical metal and soaring operatic vocals. They interpreted famous poems with The Odyssey in 2002 and Paradise Lost in 2007, the latter reaching No. 76 on the charts.

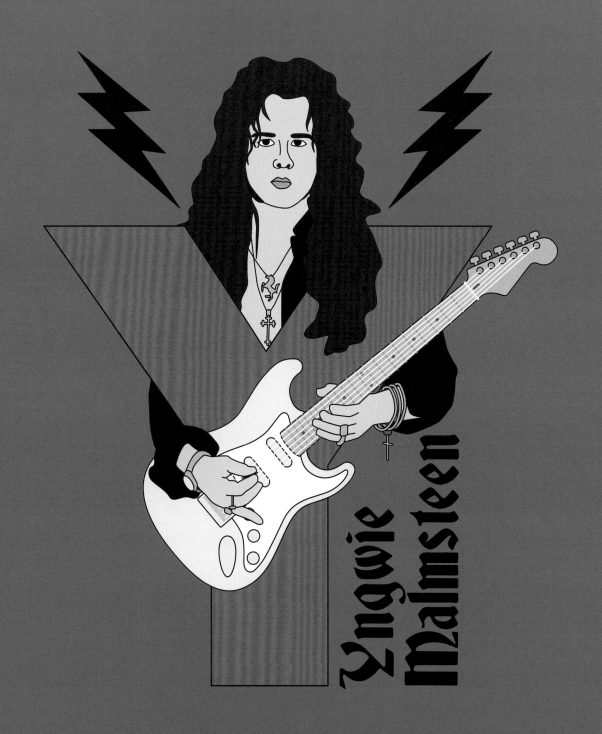

Y is for Yngwie Malmsteen.
Swedish guitar legend Yngwie Malmsteen has been revered for his speed, precision, and unique clash of metal and classical music for over 40 years. This Grammy-nominated 'Guitar Hero' even made Time Magazine's Top 10 Electric Guitarists list!

Z is for Led **Z**eppelin. They burst onto the London scene in '68, irresistibly mixing heavy blues guitar, wailing vocals, and a tantrum of drums. Page, Plant, Jones, and Bonham laid the bedrock from which headbangin' metal arose. Consequently, Rolling Stone described them as 'the heaviest band of all time.'

The ever-expanding legendary library

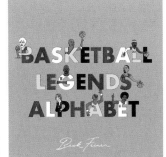

EXPLORE THESE LEGENDARY ALPHABETS & MORE AT WWW.ALPHABETLEGENDS.COM

METAL LEGENDS ALPHABET
www.alphabetlegends.com

Published by Alphabet Legends Pty Ltd in 2022
Created by Beck Feiner
Copyright © Alphabet Legends Pty Ltd 2022

9780645487015

Printed and bound in China.